Wheels, Wings, and Water

Spacecraft

Heather Miller

Heinemann Library

Chicago, Illinois

Customer Service 888-454-2279
Visit our website at www.heinemannlibrary.com

Designed by Sue Emerson, Heinemann Library; Page layout by Que-Net Media
Printed and bound in the United States by Lake Book Manufacturing, Inc.
Photo research by Amor Montes De Oca

07 06 05 04 03
10 9 8 7 6 5 4 3 2 1

Library of Congress Cataloging-in-Publication Data
Miller, Heather.
  Spacecraft / Heather Miller.
       v. cm. – (Wheels, wings, and water)
Includes index.
Contents: What are spacecraft? – What do spacecraft look like? – What are spacecraft made of? – How did spacecraft look long ago? – What is a rocket? – What is a space shuttle? – What is a rover? – What is a space station? – What are some special spacecraft? – Quiz – Picture glossary.
  ISBN 1-4034-0882-3 (HC) ,1-4034-3623-1 (Pbk.)
  1. Space vehicles–Juvenile literature. [1. Space vehicles.] I. Title. II. Series.
TL793.M55 2003
  629.47–dc21

                                    2002014726

Acknowledgments
The author and publishers are grateful to the following for permission to reproduce copyright material:
pp. 4, 15, 18 Science VU/NASA/Visuals Unlimited; pp. 5, 19 NASA/Roger Ressmeyer/Corbis; p. 6 Roger Ressmeyer/Corbis; pp. 7, 22, 24 NASA; p. 8 AFP/Corbis; p. 9 James L. Amos/Corbis; p. 10 Corbis; p. 11L AP Wide World Photos; p. 11R Corbis; p. 12 Scott Berner/Visuals Unlimited; p. 13 Science VU/NASA/JPL/Visuals Unlimited; p. 14 NASA/TRIP; p. 16 A. J. Copley/Visuals Unlimited; p. 17 NASA Langley Research Center; p. 20 NASA/Corbis; p. 21 Summer Productions; p. 23 row 1 (L-R) NASA/Corbis, Photodisc, NASA, Science VU/NASA/Visuals Unlimited; row 2 (L-R) NASA, Science VU/NASA/Visuals Unlimited, A. J. Copley/Visuals Unlimited, James L. Amos/Corbis; row 3 (L-R) Science VU/NASA/Visuals Unlimited, Corbis, Roger Ressmeyer/Corbis, Science VU/NASA/Visuals Unlimited; row 4 (L-R) Bruce Berg/Visuals Unlimited, Summer Productions; back cover (L-R) NASA/Corbis, NASA

Cover photograph by Science VU/NASA/Visuals Unlimited

Special thanks to our advisory panel for their help in the preparation of this book:

Alice Bethke, Library Consultant
Palo Alto, CA

Eileen Day, Preschool Teacher
Chicago, IL

Kathleen Gilbert,
Second Grade Teacher
Round Rock, TX

Sandra Gilbert,
Library Media Specialist
Fiest Elementary School
Houston, TX

Jan Gobeille,
Kindergarten Teacher
Garfield Elementary
Oakland, CA

Angela Leeper,
Educational Consultant
North Carolina Department
of Public Instruction
Wake Forest, NC

Some words are shown in bold, **like this.**
You can find them in the picture glossary on page 23.

Contents

What Are Spacecraft?

Spacecraft are **vehicles** that go into space.

They can carry people and things.

Some spacecraft go into space
without people inside.

Astronauts fly some spacecraft.

What Do Spacecraft Look Like?

nose

tail

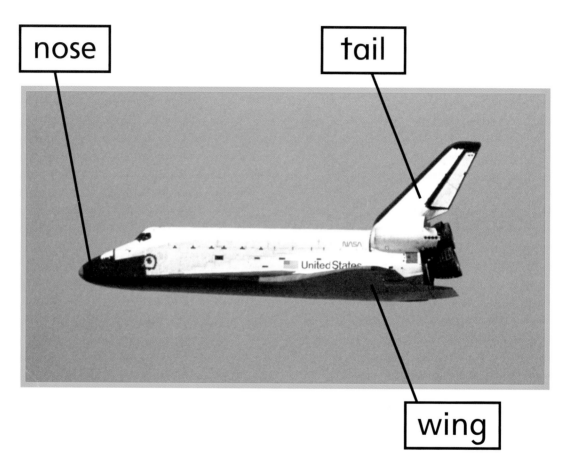

wing

Some spacecraft look like **jets**.

They have a nose, wings, and a tail.

Rockets look like tall tubes.

They have tops shaped like cones.

What Are Spacecraft Made Of?

Spacecraft have metal parts.

Scientists also make special parts to build spacecraft.

tile

Some spacecraft are covered
with special **tiles**.

They keep the spacecraft safe
from heat.

How Did Spacecraft Look Long Ago?

Early spacecraft were **capsules**.

Capsules were sent into space on big **rockets**.

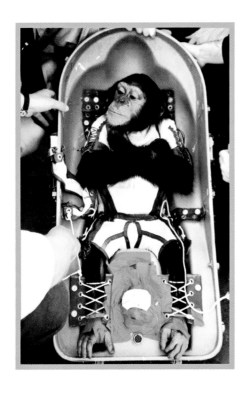

The first capsules carried animals.

Later, they carried one **astronaut**.

What Is a Rocket?

A **rocket** lifts spacecraft into space.

It is filled with fuel.

Fuel makes the rocket lift off from a **launch pad.**

Flames and smoke shoot out as the rocket launches.

What Is a Space Shuttle?

The **space shuttle** carries people and things into space.

It flies in space like a **jet.**

The space shuttle stays in space for a few days.

Astronauts fly the space shuttle back to **Earth.**

What Is a Rover?

A **rover** can drive on **planets** and the moon.

This **astronaut** is driving a rover on the moon.

Some rovers do not carry astronauts.

This rover is looking at rocks
on Mars.

What Is a Space Station?

A **space station** is a spacecraft that holds many **astronauts.**

It stays in space for a very long time.

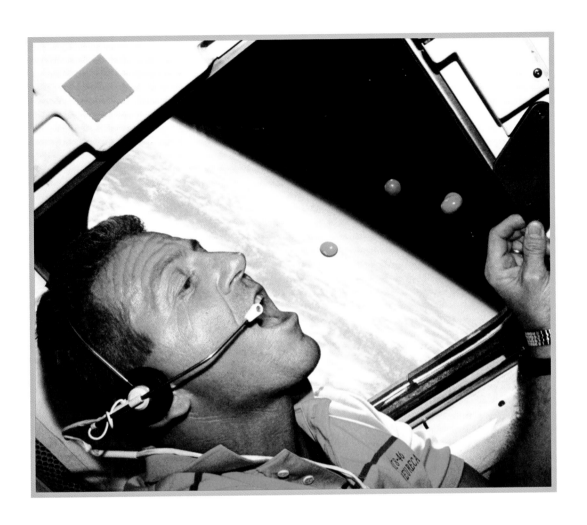

Astronauts can live and work on a space station.

This astronaut is eating in space.

What Are Some Special Spacecraft?

Jetpacks are spacecraft that help **astronauts** move in space.

Astronauts wear jetpacks on their backs.

Probes are spacecraft that take pictures of **planets.**

People cannot ride in probes.

Quiz

Do you know what kind of spacecraft this is?

Can you find it in the book?

Look for the answer on page 24.

Picture Glossary

astronaut
pages 5, 11,
15–16, 18–20

jetpack
page 20

rocket
pages 7, 10,
12

space station
page 18

capsule
page 10

launch pad
page 13

rover
pages 16–17

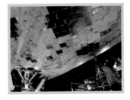
tile
page 9

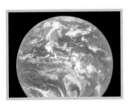
Earth
page 15

planet
pages 16, 21

**space
shuttle**
page 14

vehicle
page 4

jet
pages 6, 14

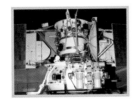
probe
page 21

23

Note to Parents and Teachers

Reading for information is an important part of a child's literacy development. Learning begins with a question about something. Help children think of themselves as investigators and researchers by encouraging their questions about the world around them. Each chapter in this book begins with a question. Read the question together. Talk about what you think the answer might be. Read the text to find out if your predictions were correct. Think of other questions you could ask about the topic, and discuss where you might find the answers. In this book, the picture glossary symbol for vehicle is a spacecraft. Explain to children that a vehicle is something that can move people or things from one place to another. Some vehicles have motors, like cars, but others do not.

Index

Answer to quiz on page 22
This is a rocket.